Birds
of prey

JILL BAILEY

Facts On File Publications
New York, New York • Oxford, England

Library of Congress Catalog Card Number:

88-450-88

Designed and produced by BLA Publishing Limited,
East Grinstead, Sussex, England.

A member of the **Ling Kee Group**
LONDON·HONG KONG·TAIPEI·SINGAPORE·NEW YORK

Phototypeset in Britain by BLA Publishing/Composing Operations
Colour origination by Waterden Reproductions
Printed and bound in Italy by New Interlitho

10 9 8 7 6 5 4 3 2 1

Note to the reader
On page 59 of this book you will find the glossary. This gives brief explanations of
words which may be new to you.

Contents

598.91
BAI

Rulers of the skies

The birds of prey are among the fiercest, the most powerful birds alive today. They live by killing and eating other animals, so they have to be very strong. All birds of prey have heavy hooked beaks and large feet with strong curving talons (big claws). They use their feet to grasp their prey and often to kill it, too. The hooked bill is used for tearing off strips of flesh to swallow, and is sometimes used for killing. Owls, which usually swallow their prey whole, have smaller beaks, half hidden in their fluffy faces.

► A symbol of power and strength, the bald eagle is the national bird of the United States.

◄ The boreal or Tengmalm's owl lives in northern coniferous forests.

Hunters large and small

Eagles are among the largest birds in the world. Some of them measure over 9 feet (2.8 meters) from wing tip to wing tip. The heaviest eagle on record was a female Harpy eagle called Jezebel who weighed over 26 lb (12 kg). The Andean condor, a South American vulture which can soar for hundreds of miles on its outstretched wings, has a wingspan of up to 10 feet 6 inches (3.23 meters).

At the other end of the scale, the tiny insect-eating falconets and the pygmy owls that live in the forests may be only 5 in (12 cm) long, smaller than a sparrow. They may weigh less than 2 oz (60 g), yet they are strongly built for their size and are able to kill birds twice their size.

Masters of the air

Birds of prey are found almost all over the world, from high mountains to wooded valleys, from the snowy tundra of the far north to the hot, dry deserts of America, Australia, Asia, and Africa.

Eagles, buzzards, hawks, and falcons are highly skilled flyers that hunt by day. Some soar high in the sky as they scan the ground for signs of life. Others swoop on their prey at speeds of up to 217 miles an hour (350 km an hour), or chase it skillfully in and out of the forest trees. By night, owls take over the skies, gliding silently through the air on their soft feathered wings as they search for prey.

The vultures do not usually kill their own prey, but feed off the discarded remains of other animals' kills, or on animals that have died of disease or old age. They can glide thousands of feet up in the sky for hours on end, tirelessly searching for dead or dying animals.

Giant ancestors

Ancestors of the birds of prey lived on the Earth about 50–60 million years ago. Fossils of a giant condor (a large vulture) have been found in the United States. When alive, this condor weighed about 44 lb (20 kg) and had a wingspan of more than 13 feet (4 meters). Giant condors were probably still living in the United States until about 10,000 years ago.

High flyers

Some birds of prey can fly very high. The remains of steppe eagles have been found on the South Col of Mount Everest, at a height of 24,600 feet (7,500 meters), and a griffon vulture was killed by a jet plane in Africa 35,500 feet (10,800 meters) above the ground. Eagles probably fly right over Mt. Everest, the highest mountain peak in the world.

▼ Vultures fly in from hundreds of miles away to feed at a carcass on the African savanna.

Designed to kill

Birds of prey, with their cruel beaks and large, well-armed talons, are very well designed hunters. They attack their prey from the air, either swooping down on it from above or, in the case of birds and insects, chasing it through the air. They seize the prey with their feet, and fly off with it, often without even stopping. If the prey is very large, the bird may have to land and adjust its grip, or perhaps kill the prey to stop it from struggling, before taking off again.

▲ A saw whet owl swings its legs forward and thrusts out its talons to seize its prey.

A fatal grip

The feet are very powerful. Eagles, hawks, and falcons have three toes pointing forwards and one pointing backwards. The inside toe and the hind toe are usually stronger than the others, with larger claws. These toes are used to grip the prey, while

Fluffy feet

eagle owl foot

Many birds of prey pull their kill to pieces before swallowing it. Their feet are usually bare and scaly — unfeathered feet are much easier to clean. But owls, which usually swallow their prey whole, do have feathered feet. An owls toes are also arranged differently, with two pointing forwards and two backwards.

 Owls usually hunt at night in dim light. Their toes can be spread very wide, which helps when trying to seize prey they cannot see too well. Their claws are extremely sharp, so that they can be sure to get a good grip of whichever part of their prey they touch.

the middle and outer toes are used to balance the foot when it is walking or perching. The claws can also be used to kill prey by piercing a weak spot, or by crushing it. Some birds of prey, such as falcons, may also use their beaks to break the neck of their prey.

Toes long and short

Some birds of prey have extra long or extra short toes. Birds that kill poisonous snakes have short toes to give a very firm grip on their wriggling prey. Some hawks and falcons live mainly on other birds, which they chase and catch in flight. They have very long middle toes, which give the foot a wider grip. Birds often twist and turn as the hawk or falcon attacks, so a bird catcher needs wide-spreading feet.

Feet for fishing

Fish-eaters have to deal with slippery prey which may be thrashing around. Fishing eagles have toes arranged like those of the owls, with two pointing backwards and two forwards. Fishing eagles and ospreys grab their prey with both feet at once, so there are four sharp claws on each side to hold the prey. Fishing owls do the same.

Unlike most owls, fishing owls have no feathers on their legs and feet. Not only would they get wet during the hunt, but fish scales are very difficult to remove from fluffy feathers. Fishing eagles, fishing owls, and ospreys have rough scales on the soles of their feet. These help the birds to get an even better grip on the wriggling fish.

▲ The powerful foot and claws of a golden eagle. The talons are strong enough to seize and kill mammals as large as mountain hares.

osprey foot

the short-toed eagle has short toes for gripping snakes

osprey with prey

bird-eating falcons have long toes

More about Hunting methods p 10, 11, 22, 23, 32-35 Catching snakes p 36, 37 Fishing birds p 38, 39

Beaks for all occasions

The birds of prey feed on fresh meat. Some are flesh-eaters, while others feed on insects, snails and other invertebrates. Between them, the birds of prey will eat everything from beetles and termites to dead whales and elephants, and even human refuse and feces.

▲ Birds of prey like this goshawk guard their food by spreading out their wings and lowering their heads in a threat display to warn off other birds.

Cruel beaks

Birds of prey have strong beaks for tearing at flesh or for crushing insects. The upper mandible (bill) has a hooked tip, and overlaps the lower mandible. This hook is used to tear the food apart. As you might expect, birds that hunt and kill large animals have bigger stronger beaks than those that feed on smaller birds and mammals.

Not so nosy

Owls' eyes are set right at the front of their faces to give them good three-dimensional vision. Their beaks are so strongly curved downwards that they are hard to see among the feathers. As owls have a less prominent nose than some other birds, it does not get in the way of their field of view when they are looking at close objects.

Shelling snails

Some of the kites have mastered the art of extracting snails from their shells. Their beaks are slender with a long curved upper mandible.

Snails are difficult to get out of their shells because they cling tightly to the inside of the shell with a very strong muscle. The snail kite uses its curved beak to reach inside the shell and cut this muscle. Then it is easy to pull the snail out of its shell.

Sometimes the kite will wait until the snail emerges of its own accord. It then uses its beak like a pair of curved forceps to seize it. Snail kites like to work on their snails at favorite perches. The ground below the perch becomes littered with hundreds of empty snail shells.

Bone-crushers

lanner falcon

Falcons and their close relatives, the South American caracaras, have two tooth-like points on the upper mandible. These are used like a pair of nutcrackers to break the necks of their prey. They are also useful for holding the kill. This is unusual as birds of prey normally use their powerful talons for killing and carrying.

Vandalizing vultures

When it comes to breaking into really tough shells, some of the vultures have some novel tricks. The Egyptian vulture is very partial to ostrich eggs, but it has a weak beak and it cannot hammer its way through their tough shells. Instead, the vulture will pick up stones and hurl them at the eggs until they break open.

The bearded vulture, or lammergeier, feeds on the large, heavy bones that other vultures cannot break into. The lammergeier carries the bones to a great height above a favorite rock, and then it drops them again and again until they smash open on the ground below. The vulture can then get at the rich bone

▲ Barn owl with prey. Owls use their beaks instead of their feet to carry their prey. Unlike other birds of prey, owls often swallow their prey whole.

marrow inside. Lammergeier use the same trick to break open tough tortoise shells.

▼ An Egyptian vulture uses a stone to crack open a tough ostrich egg.

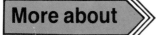

Food and feeding

It may seem cruel that birds should kill and eat other animals. In fact, the birds of prey help to keep other animal groups healthy. No bird is going to attack a fit active animal that is likely to fight back if it can take a weak sickly animal instead. So birds of prey help to remove animals that are ill. This may prevent disease spreading through a group of prey animals, and it ensures that only the strongest, fittest animals survive to produce the next generation.

Fussy feeders

Bird-eating raptors pluck their prey before eating it. Usually they have a favorite plucking post, and the ground below becomes littered with feathers. By looking at the different types of feathers you can tell what the bird has been eating.

◀ After it has eaten a large meal, the bulge of this king vulture's crop is easy to see.

Saving it for later

A buzzard may spend the whole day hunting in order to catch enough mice to feed itself, while a fish eagle may fish for less than an hour. The bat hawk catches a day's supply of food in just half an hour at dusk, killing the bats as they leave their cave homes. An eagle that kills a large antelope can devour enough food at one sitting to last it for six days, but smaller raptors, which feed on insects, need dozens of small meals just to satisfy a day's hunger.

The raptors and vultures can store food in a crop, a pouch in the stomach. This allows them to eat far more than they need at one sitting. Food stored in the crop can be regurgitated (brought back into the mouth) later, and either digested or fed to the young. After a large meal, you can see the crop bulging with food.

Owls do not have a crop, but swallow their prey whole. Some owls store food near their nest sites to eat later.

A tough diet

Birds of prey need to eat large quantities of food for their size, because as much as 30% of their food may be made up of indigestible feathers, fur or bone. The indigestible material is regurgitated some time after the meal in the form of a small pellet.

You can investigate a pellet by placing it in a small dish of water, and gently teasing it apart with a fine pair of forceps. You will find fur, bones, feathers, and the wingcases and some other hard parts of insects. There are books that will help you to identify them.

Try to find out if the content of the bird's pellets vary at different times of the year. Make your own collection by mounting the pellet contents on pieces of card. You may like to draw the pellet before you dissect it.

▲ An American kestrel chick regurgitates a pellet.

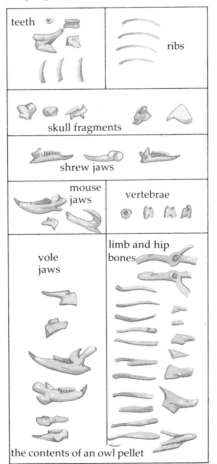

teeth

ribs

skull fragments

shrew jaws

mouse jaws

vertebrae

vole jaws

limb and hip bones

the contents of an owl pellet

Collecting bird pellets

Different kinds of birds produce different kinds of pellets, with very different shapes and contents. The pellets are easy to find as they accumulate below the bird's roosting place. Look under large trees and around barns and deserted or empty buildings.

Other birds also produce pellets. You may find crow pellets under their nesting trees, and seagull pellets beneath the cliffs where the seagulls nest.

sparrowhawk

tawny owl

rook

crow

herring gull

More about　Vultures p 6-7, 15, 22-25, 48-49 Buzzards p 14, 17, 25, 33, 51
Bat hawk p 33, 53 Bird of prey diets p 10, 11, 24, 25, 36-37, 48, 53

Living space

▲ The buzzard defends a large territory in which to hunt.

Birds of prey attract attention because they usually hunt alone, or sometimes in pairs. They need to hunt over a very large area to find enough prey. This area is called a territory. Within this territory, a pair of birds has exclusive hunting rights. If another bird strays into their territory, it will be attacked and driven off by both members of the resident pair.

A pair of Scottish golden eagles needs a territory of about 18 square miles (46 square km). Red kites, which feed on smaller mammals and birds, need a territory of about 10 square miles (25 square km).

"Whoo" goes there?

The eerie calls that owls make during hunting tell other owls where they are. Most owls defend a territory. Their calls warn other owls not to come too near. Neighboring owls will answer back, giving their own warning. If there is no answering call, an owl may assume that the nearby territory is not occupied, and that he is free to hunt there.

Pirates

Many birds of prey steal food from weaker birds if they get the chance. Even when they are not hungry, some birds will rob others. Large seabirds, such as fishing eagles, skuas, and frigatebirds, chase other seabirds and attack them in mid-air, until they are forced to drop their food to escape. Frigatebirds even steal each other's nest material and will eat each other's eggs. Young frigatebirds learn to steal before they learn to fish.

A ghostly morse code

Different kinds of owls have different calls. The tawny owl's call sounds just like "Tu-whit, tu-whoo," while the barn owl utters a loud blood-curdling screech. The screech owl's distinctive cry has been described as "Oh-o-o-o-o that I had never been bo-r-r-r-rn."

Each owl call has both long and short notes, like a morse code. Most of these calls are low-pitched, and they can be heard clearly from a long way away. For example, the snowy owl's call can travel over 7 miles (1 km).

▲ Black vultures roosting on cardon cactus in the Sonora Desert. Here, they are safe from foxes and other animals that hunt by night.

A rare social life

In areas where there is plenty of food, birds of prey may gather in large numbers. A good-sized population of locusts or termites are able to support colonies of up to 100,000 insect-eating falcons. Vultures, too, roost in groups of up to 250 birds. Where food is plentiful in supply, but uneven in distribution, it is useful to have many pairs of eyes searching for it.

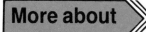
More about ⟩⟩ Roosting p 13, 40-42 Hunting calls p 29
Eagles p 6, 7, 9, 19, 22, 26, 32, 36, 40-43, 45, 51, 55, 56

Eyes of the hunter

Birds of prey have extremely sharp sight, up to eight times sharper than our eyesight. They can see us even when they are too high in the sky for us to see them. Owls can see objects in near darkness, when the light is one hundred times less bright than the dimmest light by which we can see.

▶ Birds of prey have very large eyes, which can gather a lot of light. We see only a part of the bird's eye — the rest is hidden behind the skull.

▶ Owls' eyes are set even further forward in the face, with a field of view of only 110 degrees, and an overlap of 70 degrees.

▼ Hawks have an overlapping field of view of 30–50 degrees for binocular vision, and an overall field of view of about 150 degrees.

golden eagle

Eyes forward

The main reason why birds of prey look so fierce is that they seem to stare straight at you. This is because their eyes are at the front of the head rather than the side. The fields of view of the two eyes — the area that each one can see — overlap, so the brain receives two different sets of messages about the same part of the picture. This allows the bird's brain to work out distance and speed, very important for catching prey.

European eagle owl

red-tailed hawk

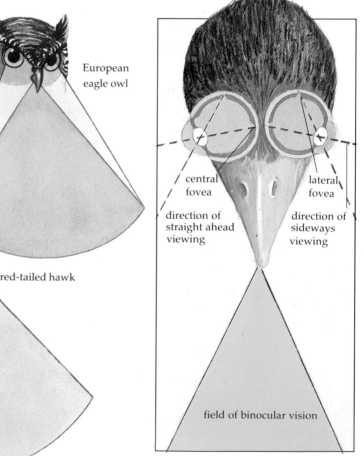

central fovea

lateral fovea

direction of straight ahead viewing

direction of sideways viewing

field of binocular vision

▲ A buzzard swoops on its prey. Buzzards glide high in the sky, scanning the ground for movement. They get up a lot of speed as they swoop down through the air, and have to swing their wings forward and spread their tail to brake.

◄ A bird of prey has a large area of overlap between the fields of view of both eyes. A second fovea gives it good vision to the side as well (see p.17).

Good all-arounders

Birds of prey also see very well to the side of their heads. Birds and mammals have an area of very densely-packed cones on the part of the retina upon which the image falls when the animals are looking straight ahead. This area is called the fovea. It explains why, if you look out of the side of your eye, you do not see as clearly as you do when you look straight ahead. Birds of prey also have a second fovea, which picks up images from objects to one side of the bird giving them good all-around vision.

Super sensors

Birds of prey have very densely packed light-sensing cells or "cones" in their eyes. The light-sensitive layer at the back of the eye, the retina, contains up to 1,500,000 cones in each square millimeter, about eight times more than we have. A buzzard can spot a grasshopper 30 feet (100 meters) away, whereas to us the insect would become invisible at about 10 feet (30 meters).

A rabbit as seen by a human from a great height. Each of the tiny squares corresponds to one light sensor on the human retina.

A rabbit as seen by a buzzard from the same height. The buzzard's eye has more closely packed light sensors than the human eye.

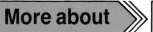

More about 〉〉

Eyesight p 18, 19, 25, 30 Hawks p 10, 18, 26, 32, 33, 35, 44, 47, 53
Owls p 8, 11, 13, 15, 18-20, 28-31, 33, 34, 40-42, 45, 49-51

Detectives at work

A look at the head of a raptor, a day-flying bird of prey, will soon tell you which senses it relies on most. The large piercing eyes dominate the head, the ears are almost invisible, and the nostrils are small and inconspicuous. The owls, which hunt mainly at night, also have large eyes, but their eyes are surrounded by huge disks of flattened feathers that act as sound collectors. Sound is much more useful than sight in very dim light.

▼ Portrait of a goshawk — the head is dominated by its large eyes.

Not so nosy

Most birds have a poor sense of smell. When hunting from on high, smell is not much use as wind currents make it very difficult to detect exactly where the smell is coming from.

The nostrils of birds of prey are placed near the top of the beak in a fleshy, often brightly colored, area called the "cere." The king vulture is one of the few birds of prey with a good sense of smell. It hunts in the dense forests of South America, and probably finds decaying animal carcasses by their smell.

long-eared owl

Hidden ears

A bird's ears are difficult to see. The so-called ears of some owls are not ears, just tufts of feathers. The true ear is an opening a little way behind the eye. The feathers around the ear can be raised to form a slight ruff. Owls have large ear openings behind their facial disks. Harriers and goshawks have small facial discs. They hunt by flying low over the ground, and probably use hearing to help them to find small mammals hiding in the long grass.

Whoo is in the dark?

Light enters the eye through the dark pupil in the center. In very bright light the pupil shrinks to protect the light-sensitive inner part of the eye. In the dark, owls can expand their pupils until they almost fill the eye. Look at the pictures of owls in this book. Can you guess which ones were photographed in the dark, and which ones in the light.

Eyes at the back of its head

A buzzard's eye is almost the same size as a human eye, yet humans are about 58 times bigger than buzzards. The eyes almost fill their sockets, and cannot swivel around. Birds of prey have very flexible necks, and turn their heads instead. An owl can turn its head almost full circle.

barn owl

Taking a good look

To judge distance even better, a bird of prey will move its head from side to side, to see or hear the object from different angles. It may even look at it upside-down, just to make sure. Because birds of prey usually hunt from the air, they have a particularly dense area of light-sensitive cells in the upper part of their retina, the part on which the image falls when looking down. So, by turning their heads upside down, they can focus the images on these cells.

Goggles for flying

Like humans, birds have upper and lower eyelids. They also have an extra eyelid in the form of a semi-transparent skin, called the nictitating membrane. This membrane can be drawn over the eye to moisten it and remove dust. It is also used to screen the eye from glare in bright sunlight, and to protect it against dust and rain when the bird is flying. The main eyelid is used only when a bird sleeps.

Owls are unusual among birds because their true eyelids are drawn down when closed. In most other birds the lower eyelids are drawn up. This makes owls look more like humans.

▼ An Imperial eagle uses its third eyelid or "nictitating membrane" to protect its eye.

More about ≫ Hearing and listening p 14, 15, 29, 31, 34, 45
Hunting at night p 14-16, 28-31 King vulture p 12, 25

Patrolling the skies

▲ Barn owl in flight.

There are many different ways of flying, and the birds of prey have mastered just about every one of them. There are birds that can travel for miles without even flapping their wings, and birds that can flap their wings so fast that they are able to hover in mid-air. Some birds of prey rise with ease upward for thousands of feet on warm, spiraling currents of air. Other hunting birds can dive swiftly through the air at speeds of up to 217 miles an hour (350 km an hour).

Flappers

Normal flight relies on flapping. The wings do not simply flap up and down. As the wing beats down, it twists at the wrist so that it pushes the air both down and back — this gives the bird "lift," which makes it rise in the air, and "thrust," which propels it forward. As the wing is raised, it folds at the wrist so that it offers little resistance to the air.

Notice what happens to the feathers. Most of the work is done by the primary feathers — the long flight feathers. When the wing beats down, the feathers are kept close together, giving a much larger surface to push against the air. But as the wing rises, the feathers spread out, and the air rushes through. If this did not happen, the upstroke would push the bird back down again.

Hovering

When a bird hovers, its wings make a sort of figure of eight, beating down and forward on the downstroke, and down and back on the upstroke. Thus the bird moves neither forward nor backward, but gets lift on both strokes to compensate for not getting up any speed. The body is held at a steep angle, so that the wings beat forwards and backwards rather than up and down. The head remains in the same position, allowing the bird to focus on its prey.

Larger birds like buzzards hover by flying into the wind at the same speed that the wind blows them backwards. This means that they remain in exactly the same place.

swallow-tailed kite

Aerial acrobats

Birds like swallows and swifts can fly extremely fast when chasing insects, but they have to slow up to approach a nest site or to seize an insect. These birds have forked tails which are closed when they are flying at high speed, but which spread out at slower speeds to help the bird to glide, steer, and brake. The swallow-tailed kites are almost as agile as the swallows themselves when chasing insects, and have similar forked tails.

▲ A kestrel hovers as it prepares to swoop on its prey.

Wheeler dealers

Birds like falcons and kites, which chase and kill other birds in flight, and the forest falcons (right), which hunt among trees, need to be able to make very rapid and accurate twists and turns. As they do not fly fast for long distances, they usually have rather short rounded wings. However, they have long tails for steering.

Shaped for speed

Birds of prey rely on skillful flight for catching their prey. Not only do they have to swoop fast and accurately, but the prey may try to escape at the last minute, so fast twists and turns are also needed. The sleek shape of birds of prey helps them slip through the air easily. Their smooth outline is due to a thick coating of feathers, which adds to their powerful appearance. Feathers may make up over half of the body weight of the bird.

When a bird is flying, it tucks up its legs and holds its head out straight. If viewed from the side, its body is torpedo-shaped — "streamlined." This shape offers least air resistance.

More about Streamlining p 33 Barn owls p 11, 15, 19, 29, 31, 34 Hovering p 32, 38 Kites p 10, 14, 27, 33, 35, 51, 55

Lazy flyers

Many birds of prey can glide for long distances without flapping their wings. They rely on flapping to get them up to a reasonable height, then they glide gently down. Birds like the harriers, which fly rather slowly not far above the ground, also use wind currents to help keep them airborne as they glide. They fly into the wind and the slight updraft of air stops them from losing height too quickly. This kind of gliding is called "soaring."

Riding on air

Gliding and soaring birds usually have long broad wings and large fat tails. When gliding, the tail is often spread out like a fan, and the bird can steer by altering the tilt of its tail, or by twisting or tilting its wings. Often the long feathers at the tips of the wings are spread out to help reduce air resistance. This is particularly useful at low speeds of flying, as it helps to prevent the bird from stalling.

Sky-diving

Many raptors rely on a high-speed dive to surprise their prey. They swoop down swiftly by raising their wings at a steep angle, so that the air rushes up past them. At the last minute, the tail spreads out and the wings swing forward to brake, as the talons reach for the kill. Birds like the falcons, which rely on high speed to overtake their prey, have long narrow-tipped wings for extra speed.

▼ This white-backed vulture has the long narrow wings typical of a soaring bird of prey.

a martial eagle surprises its prey

► Vultures make use of rising warm air currents to spiral higher and higher above the immense African plains.

▼ A peregrine dives out of the sky to snatch its prey in mid-air.

Record-breaking peregrine

The peregrine is the master diver. It folds its wings close to its body, tilts its head down and drops like a bullet, reaching speeds of up to 217 miles an hour (350km an hour) and knocking its prey out of the sky.

High flyers

Some gliding birds reach great heights by using air currents. Once air warms up in the sun, it rises creating warm spiraling drafts of air called thermals. Air also rises where it is blown against a hill or cliff. Soaring birds like vultures launch themselves from a cliff into a thermal and glide. As long as the air is rising faster than the bird is sinking, the bird will rise too.

The larger the bird, the stronger the thermal it needs to keep it aloft. Small vultures can start hunting much earlier in the morning than large ones, which must wait for the stronger thermals that develop as the land warms up.

Once it reaches the top of the thermal, the bird can glide gently down, often traveling for several miles until it reaches another thermal and starts to rise again. This mode of travel allows large birds of prey like eagles and buzzards to make long migrations without becoming exhausted.

More about ▷ Soaring and gliding p 25, 34, 47, 45, 51 Swooping on prey p 8, 31-33, 38, 39 Peregrines p 26, 41, 52, 56

The vultures

By human standards, the vultures are the scruffiest of the birds of prey. With their ruffled feathers, their scrawny necks and often red-flushed faces, they look very much like a bunch of tramps.

Vultures are some of the largest birds of prey. The Andean condor from South America is the largest one of all. It is up to 3ft 10in (1.5 meters) long and weighs over 25lb (11kg).

Vultures belong to two different families. The group called the Cathartids are found only in North and South America. All the other vultures in the world belong to the Accipitrid family, which includes hawks and eagles.

Designed for scrounging

Vultures spend a lot of time soaring high up in the sky, looking for dead or dying animals. Vultures have long wings which help them to stay airborne with very little effort, and give them a hunched up appearance when at rest.

Since they spend some time on the ground chasing other vultures away from their dinner, vultures have feet shaped like chickens feet, well suited to walking and running. With their long wings and heavy bodies, vultures have to make quite a long take-off run to launch themselves into the air.

A gruesome diet

Vultures feed on carrion (animal corpses), although some vultures will kill for themselves from time to time. Their diet explains their odd appearance. Vultures have to thrust their heads and necks inside bloody carcasses, and blood-stained feathers would be very difficult to clean. So their heads and necks are often almost bare, or covered only with tufts of down or bristles. Some vultures have ruffs of feathers around their necks, which perhaps prevents the rest of the body from getting soiled. Despite their rather messy feeding habits, vultures are very clean birds, and bathe frequently.

Egyptian vulture

◄ Two lappet-faced vultures survey the African savanna.

Funny faces

Some vultures have very bright red, yellow or orange faces, sometimes with strange fleshy flaps of skin, called wattles, hanging from them. The lappet-faced vulture has a pair of reddish wattles, or "lappets," which resemble drooping ears. The king vulture has a bright orange neck, yellow skin behind the eye, purple wattle hanging in front of its eye, and a huge swollen bright orange flap of skin that droops down over its beak. These colors are probably used during courtship displays.

▲ A turkey vulture spreads its wings to sunbathe in the hot, dry Sonora Desert.

Riding high

Most vultures find their food by sight. It is always pretty surprising how very large numbers of vultures seem to appear out of an empty sky after an animal has died. They fly in from miles around, often even before the animal is completely dead.

Vultures have very keen eyesight, and can probably spot a carcass from a height of 9,850–13,133 feet (3,000–4,000 meters) in the air. At this height, a human standing on the ground cannot even see the vultures in the sky. A vulture also looks out for other vultures in the distance.

If they start to descend, it knows there is a carcass nearby. As it, too, descends, vultures from even further away see it and follow.

The flying dustmen

Because of their gruesome diet, vultures are extremely useful birds. They clean up decaying carcasses in a very short time so that no rotting flesh is left lying around to spread disease.

In those parts of the world where there are no refuse collectors, vultures often come into cities and feed on human refuse. They will even eat feces.

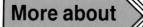

More about ⟩⟩ Eating carrion (dead flesh) p 7, 27, 53, 54 Birds in cities p 52, 53, 56 Vultures p 6, 7, 11, 12, 15, 18, 22-27, 42, 43, 48, 49, 54 ⟩

The raptors

There are many different kinds of birds of prey, but they fall into two main groups: those that hunt by day, the raptors, and those that hunt by night, the owls. There are 286 different kinds of raptors, and 133 different owls. The raptors include the hawks, buzzards, kites, eagles, the osprey, vultures, falcons, and the secretary bird. They are found in most parts of the world.

Hunters big and small

Raptors range from huge eagles to tiny falconets no bigger than the European songthrush. They feed on everything from beetles to calves and lambs, and from human refuse to the remains of dead elephants and whales.

The fierce expression of most raptors is due to a ridge of bone just above the eye. Just in front of the eye is a patch of skin bare of feathers, but covered in stiff bristles. This also makes the eye look fiercer. Ospreys, large fish-eating eagles, lack this bony ridge over the eyes and so they form a separate group of their own.

Recognizing raptors

You can recognize the main groups of raptors by the shape of their wings and tail when flying, the type of flight, and the color and pattern of their feathers. Below, you will find a quick check list of the main groups of raptors.

Buzzards

common buzzard

☆ **Broad, almost rectangular, wings.**
☆ **Feathers at wingtips usually separated to look like a fringe.**
☆ **Tail often spread out fan-like in flight.**
☆ **Wings straight, with a slight curve at wrist.**
☆ **Legs usually scaly.**

Eagles

golden eagle

☆ **Similar shape to buzzard, but longer wings.**
☆ **Legs covered in feathers almost to the toes.**
☆ **Some eagles have a crest of feathers on their heads which they can raise to threaten or display to their mates.**

Falcons

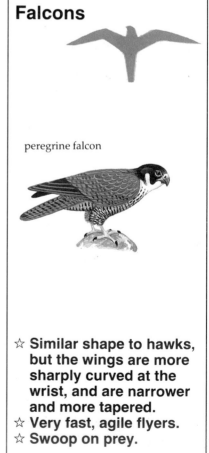

peregrine falcon

☆ **Similar shape to hawks, but the wings are more sharply curved at the wrist, and are narrower and more tapered.**
☆ **Very fast, agile flyers.**
☆ **Swoop on prey.**

Lazy caracaras

The caracaras are strange-looking falcons that live in North and South America. Like the vultures, caracaras have patches of bare, brightly colored skin on their faces. They feed more on carrion than on prey that they have caught and killed themselves.

The vegetarian vulture

There is one raptor which feeds mainly on palm nuts and dead fish. The palm nut vulture is really a fish eagle, but lives only where oil palms and raffia palms grow. It even nests in the middle of a cluster of palm nut

The snake-eating secretary

The long-legged secretary bird is not closely related to other raptors, and looks more like a stork. It hunts for snakes on the ground. The name comes from the black-tipped plumes at the back of its head, which were thought to look like old-fashioned quill pens tucked behind the ears.

common caracara

secretary bird

Harriers

hen harrier

☆ **Long-legged birds.**
☆ **Long, curved, tapering wings with upturned wingtips and long tails.**
☆ **Usually glide low over the ground.**

Kites

red kite

☆ **Similar to harriers, smaller but with longer forked tails.**
☆ **They spend a lot of time soaring.**
☆ **They also hover.**

Hawks

sparrowhawk

☆ **Moderately long legs, short, rounded wings and long tail.**
☆ **Fly at high speed at low level to chase prey.**

More about ➤➤ Secretary birds p 36 Harriers p 18, 22, 27, 34, 42, 44, 46
Falcons p 8, 9, 11, 15, 22-23, 32, 33, 42, 43, 49, 52, 55, 56

The owls

With their ghost-like appearance and large staring eyes, owls have probably been feared ever since humans first heard their eerie calls in the darkness. The Romans and some of the American Indians believed the owl to be an omen of destruction and death. The ancient Arabs thought that owls represented the souls of murdered people who had died unavenged.

Owls have many human-like features. They have large faces with big forward-looking eyes, and upper eyelids that can blink, unlike those of other birds. Many owls have tufts of feathers that resemble ears. Their beaks are small, and at first glance look almost like a nose. An owl usually stands upright on its large feet, like a little old man in a thick, cuddly coat.

▲ The screech owl looks like a little old man.

Hunted round the clock

Owls are almost as varied as the raptors in their feeding habits and hunting techniques. They form the night shift of the birds of prey. There are huge eagle owls, up to 2 ft 4 in (73 cm) long and 5.5 lb (2.5 kg) in weight. These are the nocturnal equivalent of the large eagles. The pygmy owls and elf owls match the tiny falconets, and the fishing owls compare with the osprey and the fish eagles. In fact, the largest owl is 100 times the weight of the smallest.

▲ The snowy owl lives in the Arctic regions of Europe, Asia, and North America. The male has a snow-white plumage which blends with the winter landscape. The female's plumage is barred with mottled grey bands, to match the rocks among which she nests.

Day-flying owls

Not all owls fly by night. In fact, even night-flying owls probably see better than we do by day, except that they do not have good color vision. Owls like the snowy owl, which live in the far north where the summer nights are very short or non-existent, have to hunt by day, at least for part of the year. The tiny pygmy owls also hunt by day, and are often mobbed by other birds.

Soft talk

The owls are the only birds of prey to use sound a lot for communicating with each other. Most birds use color and pattern and displays to recognize each other, attract mates, and threaten or calm down opponents. But owls have to do much of their communicating in the dark. Instead of visual signals, they use a whole range of sounds — clicks, moans, screeches, hoots, grunts, snores, barks, hisses, and whispers to express their feelings. The call can tell another owl about the caller's age and sex, as well as its message and position.

Loud calls are used when the owls are hunting and when they are alarmed, softer calls are used for begging and courting. When they are threatened, owls will click their beaks as a warning. Courting couples sometimes sing a duet, each bird with its own special phrase.

▲ A little owl arrives at its nest hole. The little owl can often be seen in the early morning or late afternoon. Despite its short tail, it will sometimes hover as it searches for insects.

Barn owls are different

The barn owls and the bay owls belong to a different family from the other owls. They are easily recognized by their heart-shaped faces. Barn owls are also unique in having combs on their middle claws, and their wishbones fused to their breastbones. When perching, they tend to look knock-kneed.

bay owl

More about ⟫ Owl courtship p 45, Owl homes p 42, 43, 49, 52
Mobbing p 41 Screech owl p 49 Pygmy Owl p 6, 46

Designed for darkness

Owls hunt mainly at night, and in the dim light of dawn and dusk. Smaller owls feed on night-flying insects, larger ones on small mammals and birds — including other owls. In fact, owls do not hunt in total darkness, although they can navigate by hearing alone. But they can see in extremely dim light. An owl has been known to catch a mouse inside a large barn when the only light available was moonlight filtering through a small crack in the wall.

Night eyes

Owls have even bigger eyes than the other birds of prey. They are so large that there is no room to move them in their sockets. If an owl wants to see to the side or behind itself, it has to turn its head. But owls have extremely flexible necks, and can turn their heads through almost a full circle. They can also turn their heads upside down.

These large eyes can gather a lot of light, which helps the owl to see in dim light. They are almost tubular in shape, and work something like binoculars, which are good at collecting light. Like binoculars, they have a rather narrow field of vision, only about 110 degrees. They also have a limited range of focus, since an owl does not need

long-distance vision. If an owl wants to see clearly what it is eating, it has to draw its head back to focus on its food.

▼ A long-eared owl looks you full in the face. Owls' eyes can see even in very dim light.

Shining eyes

If you shine a light at an owl at night, its eyes will reflect gold or yellow. This is due to a special layer at the back of the eye, the tapetum, which reflects light back into the eye, so that more light hits the retina.

The sound of supper

The owl also relies on hearing the squeaks and rustles of its prey. Owls are much better at working out the direction of sounds than we are. The large flattened discs of feathers that surround an owl's eyes are thought to act as sound reflectors, directing the sound to the ears just behind them.

The barn owls, with their strange heart-shaped faces, have one ear set higher than the other. This means that the two ears not only receive the sound from a different angle in the horizontal direction, but they can also detect differences in the vertical direction. This helps the owl to locate the sound.

When using its eyes to find its prey, an owl will glide confidently towards its prey on outstretched wings. But if it is using its ears alone, it flaps its wings, keeping its head lined up with its prey until the last moment, when it swings its legs and talons forward to snatch the prey.

▲ Barn owls have pale, heart-shaped faces.

▼ A barn owl sets out to hunt at sunset.

Softly, softly

Surprise is important in catching prey at night. Owls have special soft fringes along the edge of their flight feathers to muffle the sound of their approach. Even their feet are feathered, and make no noise as they swing into action for the kill.

The art of surprise

For a bird of prey, its hunting skills are the key to its survival. Many young birds die within a few months of leaving home because they do not learn to hunt well enough.

"Still hunting"

Many birds of prey hunt from a look-out post, either a tall tree or a cliff which gives a good view of the surrounding countryside. Telephone poles are popular perches, since prey animals are easily seen as they attempt to cross the road. Once it has spotted its prey, the bird swoops on it from behind, relying on speed and surprise to catch it. Eagles, hawks, and falcons "still hunt," catching prey of all sizes from grasshoppers to monkeys. Many owls hunt in this way; they rely on both seeing and hearing their prey moving below. "Still hunting" works well in forests as it does not require a long unhindered flight.

◄ A harpy eagle swoops down from its look-out perch to surprise an agouti. One of the rarest birds of prey, the harpy eagle lives in the South American jungles.

Soar and swoop

Large birds like buzzards and eagles can soar at great heights on the air currents. They scan the ground from three thousand feet or more up, then they swoop down very rapidly, gaining so much speed that they often kill their prey outright with a single blow from the feet. Such a high-speed swoop is called a "stoop."

Falcons and kites can get up great speeds as they hunt birds and insects, sometimes overtaking their prey and attacking it from below. Many falcons and kites have relatively long legs to extend their reach. These smaller, lighter birds are extremely agile flyers, twisting and turning with ease. The hobby can even fly fast enough to capture swifts in flight.

The bat-catcher

The bat hawk of southern Africa and Indonesia is the only bird of prey that specializes in eating bats. It hunts only at dawn and dusk, when the bats leave their cave homes. The bat hawk looks and flies like a high-speed falcon, seizing the bats with its long claws. It then swallows the bats whole while still in flight. This saves time and allows it to catch most of its daily ration in just half an hour.

◀ Like this hobby, most birds of prey have very sleek stream-lined bodies.

▼ A great gray owl sits on its favorite perch, on the look-out for prey.

Hunters fast and slow

Some birds of prey rely on a swift attack from above to surprise their prey. Others glide quietly overhead, stalk their prey on foot through the long grass, or reach into burrows with their long legs.

Flap and glide

In open country and marshes, where there are no perches and where long grass or reeds conceal the prey, a bird of prey needs to hunt near the ground to find its prey. Long-winged lightweight birds, such as harriers, barn owls, and short-eared owls, glide a few feet above the ground. They flap their wings every few seconds to help to maintain their height. In this way, they are able to surprise insects, frogs, small birds, and rodents.

The same tactic is used by large forest eagles that glide over the tops of jungle trees. They snatch whole nests and carry them off to eat the eggs and nestlings.

The harriers and savanna hawks have long legs for seizing prey deep down in the grasses and reeds. They also have flattened discs of feathers on their faces, rather like those of the owls, which may act as sound receivers. In long grass, it can be useful to listen, as well as to watch, for prey.

Hunting on foot

Very few birds of prey hunt on foot. They would be competing with mammals such as weasels, foxes, and wolves. But a few of the grassland hunters do hunt on the ground. They have long legs to help them reach prey in the long grass, or to see above the grasses.

The little owls and the burrowing owls of North America often bound over the ground after beetles and other insects. Spotted eagles will hunt frogs and insects on the ground, and the secretary birds of the African savannas walk several miles a day in search of snakes.

▼ A Montagu's harrier flies low as it hunts.

Flexi-knees

Harrier hawks and crane hawks have strange double-jointed legs for reaching into tree holes in search of bats, lizards, eggs, and young birds. They bend their knees backwards to cling to the edge of a hole as they reach inside with the other leg.

Fire followers

Kites and other insect-eaters follow grassland fires to catch insects that are flushed out of the burning grass. American white-tailed buzzards hunt over cane fires to catch lizards and rodents as they flee from the flames.

▲ A harrier hawk investigates a tree hole.

▲ The great gray shrike stores its food on sharp thorns.

Butcherbirds

The birds of prey are not the only hunters in the bird world. The shrikes, small to medium-sized birds, hunt large insects, small mammals, frogs, and lizards by swooping down on them from look-out points, or hovering over the open grassland.

Like the birds of prey, shrikes have hooked bills for killing and tearing their prey, and strong feet for holding it. But shrikes and Australian magpies have one habit which has given them the nickname of "butcherbird." They store their prey for later by impaling it on a spike such as a thorn or a piece of barbed wire.

More about ⟩⟩ Burrowing owls p 42 Little owls p 29, 56
Secretary bird p 26, 27, 36

Eating poison

Some birds specialize in eating snakes, while others favor a diet of bees and wasps. Yet they do not appear to suffer from the stings and poisons, either while catching their prey, or while eating it.

The snake catchers

Many birds of prey will take small snakes when they find them, but a few birds actually seem to *prefer* eating snakes. Snake eagles take no notice of any other kind of food but, if a piece of rope is wiggled in front of them, they will immediately get very excited. The secretary bird of the African plains stamps very vigorously on clumps of grass to scare the snakes into showing themselves.

Snakes are not so difficult to kill as you might imagine. Their backbones are very fragile, and it is quite easy to break their necks with a sharp blow from the talons, after which the rest of the body becomes completely limp and lifeless. The snake specialists, such as the snake eagles and short-toed eagles, often have special short thick toes for grasping thin snakes.

▼ The secretary bird stalks snakes through the long grass of the African plains.

▲ The bateleur eagle often eats snakes. When alarmed or angry, the bateleur raises a crest of feathers on its head. This makes it look much bigger and fiercer.

Avoiding the poison

Snake venom will poison birds of prey just as it will poison you or me. But snake venom only works if it gets into a bird's bloodstream. If a bird swallows a poisonous snake, then the venom is digested and made harmless.

Even so, most snake-eaters cut off the snake's head before they eat it, leaving behind the poisonous fangs in the process. Then they swallow the rest of the snake whole, head first. A really large snake may be torn to pieces first.

Birds that feed on snakes have tough scales on their legs, which would be difficult to bite through. During a battle with a big snake, the snake tries to bite the bird's body, but usually it will just get a mouthful of feathers.

Bigger battles

Large, extremely poisonous snakes like rattlesnakes and puff adders must present a challenge even to the big snake eagles. The usual tactic is to tire out the snake by swooping and striking at it. Eventually the snake is so exhausted from striking back that it is an easy kill for the eagle. Laughing falcons rely entirely on surprise, swooping down unseen from their overhead perch.

Braving the bees

A few birds specialize in eating bees and wasps. The honey buzzard does not really feed on honey. It is looking for the wasps' combs and the tasty grubs inside. It follows wasps back to their nest, then digs up the nest. The honey buzzard will even snatch whole hornet and wasp nests from under the

▲ The honey buzzard steals the combs of wasps and bees to feed on the grubs inside.

eaves of houses. Special scaly skin in front of its eyes help to protect it from stings.

The colorful bee-eater is the real specialist at eating bees and wasps. It sits on favorite perches such as telephone wires and poles, waiting for bees, wasps, and hornets to fly past, then it darts out and gives chase, catching them in its beak.

The bee-eater takes its prey back to its perch, and beats the bee's head on the perch to kill it. Next, it picks up the bee or wasp by the tip of its tail and rubs it against the perch, rather as you would use a pencil eraser. This squeezes out the poison, and often removes the sting and poison bags as well. This done, the bee-eater tosses the insect into the air and swallows it whole.

◄ A European bee-eater needs 225 bees a day to feed itself and its young.

More about 》》 Snake eaters p 9, 26, 27, 34 Stealing food p 15
Food and feeding p 10-13, 24, 25, 35, 37, 44, 47, 48

Flying fishermen

Some of the most powerful birds of prey specialize in catching fish. Skilled fishermen like the osprey, the sea eagles, and the fishing eagles of the Far East, can catch such large fish that they need to spend only a few hours a day hunting. Ospreys are so successful that they are found almost all over the world, except near the poles.

The master fishermen

Like other birds of prey, the fishermen use their feet to catch their prey. Sometimes they watch from a nearby tree, but often they fly and hover above the water, then drop on to their prey, feet first, folding their wings as they enter the water. The osprey can even close its nostrils to protect its lungs from the rush of water. It can reach fish almost three feet below the surface. The fish is carried off slung, rather like a torpedo, below the eagle's body. Fishing owls hunt in the same way.

Only the osprey will actually submerge itself to catch a fish. Sometimes ospreys make mistakes — they try to take fish too big for them. Large fish have been caught with the skeleton of an osprey clinging to their backs.

▲ The osprey snatches fish from the water with its talons.

A shoal at a time

There are many other skilled fishermen in the bird world. The pelican has a stretchy throat pouch which allows it to catch lots of fish at once. The pelican opens its beak and uses the pouch like a scoop. Then it throws back its head, and swallows the fish whole.

▲ Terns hover as they search for fish in the water below.

Plunge fishing

There are many skilled bird divers — gannets, boobies, pelicans, and terns. Some, like the terns, can hover just as well as a kestrel while they scan the water below. They fold their wings until they are almost arrow-shaped and then they drop from a height into the water, swooping on their prey. But only the birds of prey use their feet to catch fish. Other fishing birds use their beaks.

Watch and wait

European kingfisher

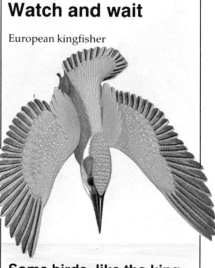

Some birds, like the kingfishers and herons, prefer to hunt by stealth. They watch the water from a favorite perch, then swoop on a fish as it swims below, spearing it with their long pointed beaks. Then they toss the fish to position it length-wise in the bill, and swallow it head first.

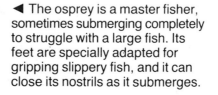

◄ The osprey is a master fisher, sometimes submerging completely to struggle with a large fish. Its feet are specially adapted for gripping slippery fish, and it can close its nostrils as it submerges.

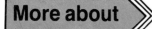

More about ⟩⟩ Ospreys p 9, 26, 48, 52, 53 Fishing p 9
Hunting methods p 8-11, 22, 23, 32-37

Enemies, defenses, and diseases

Birds of prey seldom die of disease, except when they are very old, when illnesses like pneumonia affect them just as they affect elderly humans. More commonplace problems are injuries caused during hunting or being caught by other predators.

Fluff or bluff?

When resting, owls often fluff up their feathers for warmth. Some owls, if disturbed, flatten their feathers and draw their wings close to their bodies, so that they look like stumps of wood.

Most birds of prey have special threat postures. They snap their beaks, fluff up their feathers, and raise their wings, so that they look much bigger than they really are. Some, like the bataleur eagle, have special crests of feathers on their heads that they can raise to look really fierce. Their main weapons, the talons, are thrust forwards towards the enemy.

▲ The long-eared owl can flatten its feathers and stretch its body until it resembles a tree stump.

▼ The long-eared owl puts on an impressive display when annoyed or threatened. Compare it with the display (right) it uses when trying to look part of the scenery.

Sleeping in safety

Even fierce predators like the owls have their enemies, mainly other birds of prey, including other, larger owls. Those that roost in the open rely on camouflage and on keeping still for safety. Most owls have mottled brown and gray plumage, which blends well with the trees they roost in. Desert owls tend to be a sandy color, while the snowy owl of Arctic regions is white.

Chased by the mob

Smaller birds will often mob a bird of prey, dive-bombing it and calling noisily. This behavior alerts other animals to the danger, and often irritates the bird of prey so much that it flies away. Owls especially suffer from this because they roost out in the open by day.

Death from ignorance

Many birds of prey die in their first year, usually from lack of experience. Clumsy hunting moves and collisions with branches may damage a bird's talons or wings, making it unable to catch enough prey. Unsuitable roosting sites expose it to attacks by other predators.

Wear and tear

Injuries to talons and claws are common. The talons often strike the prey with such force that the skin splits, and becomes infected. In old birds, the beaks may grow unevenly, and this makes feeding impossible.

Killed by chemicals

A new threat comes from the insecticides — chemicals sprayed on the land to kill insect pests. These will find their way into the bodies of animals that eat the poisoned insects. In turn these animals are eaten by birds of prey. The main effect is to make the egg shells very thin, so that they break when the bird sits on them to incubate them. In large doses, insecticides may poison the adult birds, or make them infertile (unable to breed).

The eagle on the flag

The eagle is often pictured on shields and flags in a typical threat posture, with their talons thrust forward.

▼ A broken peregrine egg. When birds of prey have been poisoned by insecticides, they produce eggs with thin shells that break as the parent incubates them.

More about ⟫⟫ Birds at risk p 54, 55 Displays p 36, 44, 45 Snowy owl p 28, 29, 42 Eagles p 6-9, 12-16, 19, 22-24, 26, 32, 34, 36, 38, 43, 45-47, 51, 54, 56

No place like home

When they are not out hunting, birds of prey need a safe place to rest, preen, and roost (sleep). They need an even safer place in which to nest and rear their young. Most of them build nests, or lay their eggs in hollows in trees, or on an inaccessible cliff ledge.

A place to sleep

Many raptors roost in trees, out of harm's way. If there are no trees, they may roost on buildings or cliff ledges. Birds like the harriers and snowy owls, which live in flat open country, may roost on the ground.

Most owls sleep in the daytime. Some have regular tree holes in which they roost, out of sight of other hunters. Where there are no suitable hollow trees or other sheltered crevices, owls may roost in buildings such as church towers and barns. Otherwise, they sleep out in the open, perched close to the fork of a tree.

The burrowing owls of North America, which hunt in open grasslands, live in holes in the ground. They often use the deserted burrows of prairie dogs or foxes.

▶ The burrowing owls of North America, which hunt in open grasslands, live in holes in the ground, usually in the deserted burrows of prairie dogs or foxes.

Nursery nests

Most birds of prey build nests in which to rear their young. Only the falcons and the American vultures do not make nests. The nests range from small platforms of sticks, which are used for only one season, to huge piles of sticks, big enough for a human family, which are

▲ The booted eagle's eggs rest on a soft, warm layer of freshly gathered leaves.

used year after year.

Some of the larger eagles build nests that are among the largest in the world. Many eagles use the same nest year after year, adding to it every spring. Even if one of the pair dies, the other will take a

High-rise housing

The tiny elf owls of North America live in holes in tall desert cacti, often in the abandoned nest-holes of woodpeckers. The rows of sharp cactus spines offer as good protection as a barbed wire fence.

▲ An African hawk eagle and its chick at their nest. Eagles build some of the largest nests in the world.

new mate, and continue with the same nest, sometimes for 80 years or more.

The biggest nest on record is that of a pair of bald eagles in the United States, which was used for 63 years. When it came down in a storm, it was nearly 10 feet (3 meters) wide and 20 feet (6 meters) deep, and weighed more than 2 tons (tonnes).

Nests are usually built in tall trees, on cliff ledges, or on the ground. The American vultures make no nests, but usually lay their eggs on cliff ledges, in hollow trees, in caves, or just on the ground. Many falcons use other birds' nests, sometimes driving off the original occupants.

A soft bed

Nests are often lined with leaves and grass, sometimes with fur and sheep's wool. If lining material is in short supply, raptors may use old pellets or even camel dung.

Owls do not make proper nests, but they may pile up plant material or pellets as a cushion for the eggs.

Helped by spiders
Some birds of prey coat their nests in spider's webs. The gabar goshawk even brings in webs complete with spiders, who then cover the nest in new webs.

More about

Attracting a mate

▲ A male merlin gently tucks an egg under his body to keep it warm. Birds of prey make very good fathers.

Colorful dances

The big vultures are more sedate, and they do a lot of their courting on the ground as well as in the air. They dance around each other, flapping their wings and whistling. Male condors spread their wings and arch their necks to display the colorful skin on their necks.

female European sparrowhawk

male European sparrowhawk

Most birds of prey and owls pair for life. Even species that migrate return to the same nest sites and the same mate year after year.

Powerful females

In most raptors, the females are larger than the males, and sometimes their plumage is a different color, too. Often the two birds catch different prey. The sparrowhawk male is a fast, skillful flyer, and catches small birds. The female is larger and not such an agile flyer, but she catches larger birds. So the two birds can live in the same area without competing for food. The female stays with the chicks while the male hunts, and her larger size helps her defend them. It also helps her "persuade" the male to give up the food he brings back to the nest.

Giving presents

Feeding the female is part of many courtship rituals. The extra food helps her to make the eggs. Many falcons have elaborate food-presenting ceremonies at the nest, which often involve showing off brightly colored breasts and legs. The harriers give their presents in the air. The male bird drops the food, and the female rolls over on her back mid-air to catch it.

Showing off

The raptors engage in some of the most spectacular aerial courtship displays seen in nature. The males may swoop up and down through the air, closing their wings and diving many hundreds of feet, then sweeping upwards with flapping wings again to try and impress the female. Or both partners may wheel and dive together.

Sea eagles and kites carry this a stage further. The male swoops down on the female without swerving aside, so she has to roll over and present her talons to him to avoid being hurt. Then the pair lock talons and tumble down, cartwheeling over and over with their claws locked.

Forest eagles' short wings prevent them from soaring to great heights. They circle up above the forest, then swoop down at great speed, calling loudly so that they can be heard in the forest below. Loud calls are a part of many raptor displays, and also serve to advertise the pair's territory. Day-flying owls use displays, flying in circles above the nest and clapping their wings.

Tuneful courtship

Most owls do their courting in dim light, so extravagant displays would be wasted. Instead, they use a whole range of sounds, calling, clicking bills, and grunting. Some owls sing a duet, each partner having its own distinctive "tune." The pair will preen each other, and nuzzle together side by side, bowing and gently touching bills.

▶ A pair of bald eagles lock talons and tumble through the air in a courtship display.

More about ≫ Eggs p 46-49, 54 Parental care p 37, 42, 43, 46-49 Bald eagles p 6, 43, 51
Owl courtship p 29 Sparrowhawks p 13, 27, 52

Eggs and young

▲ It is dinner time for these red kite chicks.

Compared with most other kinds of birds, the birds of prey produce very few young at a time. The baby birds of prey must be well developed when they hatch in order to be able to digest meat, so the eggs must be of a reasonable size with plenty of yolk. The chicks also need to spend a long time with their parents, even after they are fully grown, until they have learned to fly well and to hunt. Two parents would be unable to provide enough food for a large brood.

Slow breeders

Most large birds of prey lay only one or two eggs at a time, smaller birds lay three to five eggs. Birds that nest on the ground, where the young are at greater risk from predators, produce more eggs. Harriers lay up to 10, while snowy owls produce up to 15 eggs.

Where the amount of food varies a lot from year to year, birds may lay more eggs in good years. Large birds of prey may lay no eggs at all in a year when food is scarce.

First come, first serve

Most birds of prey lay their eggs at intervals of one to four days. The female starts sitting on the eggs (incubating them) from the moment the first one is laid. This means that the young hatch at different times, and some are bigger than others.

In a good year, all the young will be fed and survive. But if food is scarce, the largest chicks are fed first, and the young ones starve to death, or are eaten by their hungry brothers and sisters. This may seem cruel, but it ensures that at least one young has a good chance of surviving instead of all the young birds starving to death.

▲ This martial eagle's eggs, like all birds of prey, do not hatch together.

▲ Red-tailed hawk chicks in their nest. The youngest chick is still in its baby down, but the older chicks already have their subadult plumage.

Babies with big feet

When newly hatched, the baby bird of prey is too weak to stand, or even to raise its head. It is covered in a soft coat of thin, silky down, which is soon replaced by thicker fluffier down. It looks rather like a clown, with a large baggy coat, a big colored mouth, black eyes, and huge feet. The big feet help the young to balance in the nest, and provide it with its own defense against intruders.

The dark eyes of the chicks, the gaping beaks, and the bobbing heads encourage the parents to feed them. Later, the dark eyes will turn yellow, orange or brown like their parents' eyes.

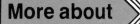

More about 〉〉
Baby birds p 13, 37, 41-43, 48, 49, 52 Red-tailed hawk p 16
Red kite p 14, 27, 53

Growing up

Baby birds of prey are luckier than many baby birds — both their parents help to bring them up. Their mother stays with them at first. She sits on the eggs to keep them warm and help them hatch faster. This is called incubation, and it can last for two to eight weeks. During this time, the male bird does all the hunting and feeds the female.

Once the eggs hatch, the baby birds still need to be kept warm until they have grown their second coat of down. Then the mother bird can leave the nest to hunt for herself, and help the male to feed the chicks. She will stay at the nest to keep them warm at night, and in cold or wet weather. If it is very hot,

▲ A black vulture shades its young from the fierce desert sun.

she will stay with the young to shade them from the sun, spreading out her wings like a sunshade.

Growing a new coat

As the chicks grow bigger, they begin to shed their baby down and start to grow proper feathers. Often this plumage is a different color from the adults. Adult colors may not come until the next molt.

Getting fatter

At first, the parents have to tear off soft pieces of meat to feed to the chicks. They will eat only the tender parts, like the heart and liver. Later, the chicks are able to cope with tougher meat like muscle, and eventually their beaks and talons are strong enough for them to tear the food up for themselves. Now their parents simply leave carcasses at the nest.

▲ This osprey chick is much smaller than the lizard its parents have brought for it to eat.

Leaving home

Eventually, the young chicks are fully feathered, and start to exercise their wings at the edge of the nest. Even after they make their first flights, they need to be fed by their parents, often for several months, while the young birds learn to hunt and kill for themselves.

If the prey is other birds, the young will have to become skilled flyers before they can hunt. The parents teach them by dropping food to them so that they can practice catching it in mid-air. They will also practice on anything that moves — falling feathers, leaves, and insects.

This is a dangerous time for the young birds, who have still to learn the signs that indicate approaching danger, and where it is safe to roost.

Most young raptors will eventually leave the nest of their own accord. But young owls are not so adventurous, and they are eventually driven away by their parents. Many will die of starvation before they manage to find a free territory of their own in which to hunt.

▲ Hunting practice for a young bat falcon.

▼ Inexperienced young screech owls are very vulnerable when they first leave home.

The oldest birds

If they survive their first year of independence, the young birds of prey have a good chance of living to a ripe old age. The vultures hold the records for the longest-lived birds. An Andean condor called Kuzya died in a Moscow zoo in 1964. It had been brought to the zoo as an adult 72 years before. In Britain, a female European eagle owl during the last century lived for more than 68 years in captivity.

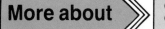

More about ❯❯❯ Coats of feathers p 20-22, 31, 36, 40, 47 Territory p 14, 45
Catching birds p 9, 23, 33 Ospreys p 9, 26, 38, 39, 52, 53 Screech owls p 28

Migration

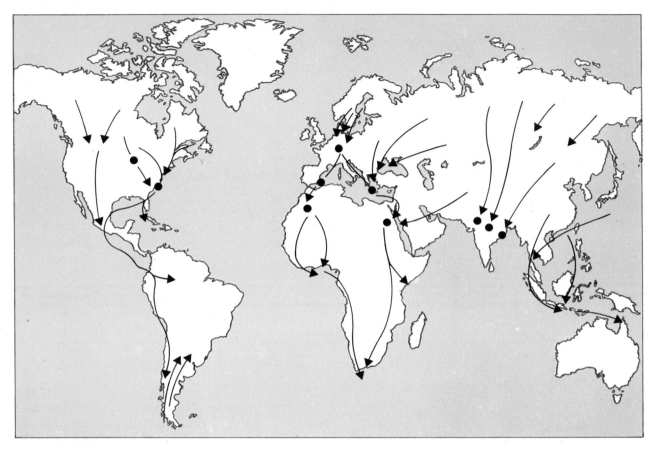

— autumn bird migration routes
● mountain, lake and sea crossing points

The birds of prey include some very experienced long-distance travelers. Some birds travel up to 10,000 miles (1,6000 km) every spring and autumn. Such regular long-distance journeys by birds are called migrations.

Long-distance travelers
About a quarter of all birds of prey migrate every spring and summer. Birds that spend summer in the far north (or far south) need to escape the severe winter there, when many of the smaller birds and animals on which they feed die or retreat to underground burrows. These birds make some of the longest known migrations. Steppe buzzards from Siberia fly to South Africa, and Swainson's hawks fly from Alaska to Argentina.

Even in temperate regions, some prey animals become unavailable in winter. Some frogs, toads, lizards, and snakes hibernate in winter.

Following the sun
The tundra is a very popular breeding ground. The very long summer days give birds extra time to hunt for food for their growing families.

Millions of insects breed in the pools left by the melting snow. These in turn attract smaller birds, themselves prey for others. The mice and voles that spent the winter hibernating underground now multiply rapidly, feeding owls, hawks, and buzzards.

Tracking migrants

Individual birds can be identified by fixing numbered metal rings on their legs. Where birds fly at very great heights, they can sometimes be tracked by radar. Shorter distance movements can be followed by attaching radio collars to birds. This can be useful for finding out where they are nesting.

Riding high

The larger migrating birds — eagles, buzzards, and some kites — use thermals to reach great heights. Then they soar gently downwards for several miles until they reach the next thermal. Thus they can travel great distances without even flapping their wings. A migrating buzzard can travel up to 150—250 miles (240–400 km) a day.

◄ This young bald eagle has been fitted with a radio collar.

▼ Ringing a sharp-shinned hawk in New Jersey.

Crossing the sea

Thermals do not form over water, so migrating birds tend to avoid lakes and sea crossings. In America, some migrating birds avoid the sea by traveling down across Central America through to the Panama Canal. But birds flying south from Europe and the USSR converge on favorite sea crossings, reaching North Africa from the tip of Spain or across the Red Sea, or island-hopping from Malaysia to places like Indonesia and Australia. Together with favorite mountain passes, these crossing points provide good observation points, so that migrating birds can be tracked by radar, counted, and ringed.

Dangerous journeys

Migration is dangerous. Weaker birds may collapse and die of exhaustion or starvation, or they may be ambushed by predators when they stop to rest. Storms and gales may blow birds off course and sap their energy. In many countries, sportsmen shoot migrating birds or snare them in nets and traps. But the gains made by traveling to special breeding areas are greater than the losses suffered on the way.

More about ►► Long-distance fliers p 22, 23, 25 Thermals p 23
Insect eaters p 12, 15, 21, 33-35, 37, 53

Birds of prey in cities

The spread of roads and cities has opened up many new opportunities for the birds of prey. Kestrels hover over highways in search of mice, and telephone poles provide good hunting perches from which to attack small animals in the short grass by the sides of roads. Bird tables in many gardens have induced the sparrowhawk, which is usually a woodland bird, to take up residence in the greener parts of suburbia. City-dwelling tawny owls in Britain now catch more birds, mostly sparrows, than mice.

New homes

There are new nesting sites for owls and raptors — church towers and derelict buildings. Window ledges on tall buildings are used instead of cliff ledges by kestrels and peregrines. Providing nesting trays for them can help, as the eggs tend to roll off sloping window ledges.

▲ Kestrel chicks in their nest on a city window ledge.

In many countries where ospreys were once common, people have put up wooden nesting platforms on tall posts. In parts of the Florida Keys, motorists can drive along roads where osprey nests on posts are almost as common as telephone poles.

Owls, feared in some countries as omens of bad luck and death, are popular birds in Europe and the United States. Many city dwellers try to encourage them to breed by providing large wooden nest boxes in secluded sites. Smaller nest boxes are used to attract peregrines and kestrels.

▲ Some birds of prey, such as kestrels, can be persuaded to use nesting boxes in city gardens.

Problems with pylons

Electricity pylons make useful perches from which to scan the surrounding countryside for prey, but the wires can electrocute birds that fly into them, mostly rather young and inexperienced flyers. In some parts of the United States, local authorities have altered the distance between the wires so that there is plenty of clearance for the wings of large birds of prey.

▼ The world's most successful birds of prey? Black kites soar over the Taj Mahal in India. They are found in large numbers in cities in the Old World tropics and subtropics, where they feed on human refuse.

Food for all

Birds of prey are useful in cities, keeping down the numbers of rats and mice. In the warmer parts of the world, scavengers like the vultures are very important for disposing of human refuse and animal carcasses, which would otherwise harbor both vermin and disease.

The black kite is probably the world's commonest and most successful bird of prey, found from Spain to Australia. It has adapted to city life, feeding on almost any food scraps as well as live prey. Being an expert at soaring, it can spot new sources of food some distance away.

In the days before modern sanitation and waste disposal, London supported a thriving population of red kites.

▲ A pair of ospreys gets a free view of the space shuttle from their nest at Cape Canaveral.

Window shopping

Some birds of prey have learned to take advantage of the misfortunes of other birds. They wait near large windows for birds that fly accidentally into the glass, then they pick them up while they are stunned — a meal for the taking. In the tropics, bat hawks hunt around the illuminated hotel windows, catching insects that are attracted to the bright lights.

More about ▶▶ Birds at risk p 40-41, 54, 55 Kites p 10, 14, 21, 26, 33, 35, 45, 46, 51, 54
Vultures p 6, 7, 11, 12, 15, 18, 22-27, 42, 43, 48, 49, 54

Birds in danger

Because they need a large area over which to hunt, most birds of prey do not occur in large numbers in any one area. But many of them are becoming rarer and rarer. The wild countryside and forests are rapidly disappearing as farms and cities grow, and with them go the birds' prey and their nesting sites.

▼ No California condors are left in the wild. It is hoped that the few in captivity can be persuaded to breed and save the species.

Too clean for comfort

Huge areas of land where large herds of grazing buffalo and antelopes once roamed have been turned into farmland. Farmers do not leave their dead animals lying about, so carrion eaters like vultures and condors are running short of food.

Other scavengers, like the kites and caracaras, also suffer from the improved sanitation and disposal of refuse in our cities.

▲ Destruction of the forests threatens the Philippine monkey-eating eagle, the world's largest raptor.

Hated by farmers

Many birds of prey are deliberately poisoned or are killed by farmers and game-keepers, who accuse them of stealing and killing young farm animals or game birds. In fact, birds of prey usually take only dead or dying animals. Similarly, fishermen see fishing eagles as their competitors. Larger owls will occasionally take young game birds or chickens. Yet many scientists have shown that most of their prey is rats and mice, which compete with game birds for food.

Slow breeders

Most birds of prey reproduce extremely slowly. They produce very few eggs and young each year, so if the adults are killed, the wild populations take many, many years to recover.

Many birds of prey lay more than one egg, although only one young bird survives. By removing the second egg and hand-rearing the chick, we can help to increase the population. This is being done with the almost extinct California condor, which produces only one chick every other year.

Where very few birds are left, some can be captured and brought together to breed in captivity where they are safe from danger and bad weather, and where there is plenty of food. If they multiply fast enough, birds can be released into the wild later. This has helped to save the rare Mauritius kestrel.

Death by poisoning

Chemicals sprayed on farmland to kill insects have poisoned many birds of prey. Many birds eat the poisoned insects and birds of prey, like

The collectors

Partly because they are already rare, many birds of prey have been captured for museums and zoos. Egg collectors have been an even worse threat. The more eggs that are taken, the rarer the bird becomes, and so the eggs will become even more valuable. Collecting eggs and birds is banned in many countries. But it is difficult to detect and stop all the collectors, especially in remote areas.

the peregrine, catch and eat these birds, which will now contain the poison.

Although the poison does not always kill the birds directly, it makes them produce eggs with very thin shells, which break before the chicks can hatch. So the birds cannot breed, and when they die, they have no offspring to replace them.

Birds that kill mammals may also die if poisoned bait is put out for pests such as rats or foxes.

▲ The Mauritius kestrel has probably been saved by breeding in captivity.

Last laugh?

The New Zealand laughing owl nests on the ground, and its eggs and young are killed by "foreign" animals such as cats and mongooses introduced by the settlers. It may already be extinct.

More about ⟫ Condors p 6, 7, 46, 49, Breeding p 42-49
Caracaras p 11, 27 Thin-shelled eggs p 41

An ancient history

Birds of prey have been associated with humans for thousands of years. They have been used as symbols of power on temples, flags, emblems, shields, and even on totem poles. Carved brass or wooden eagles are found in many churches. The bald eagle, a bird of prey, is the national bird of the United States of America.

Owls are also associated with some ancient gods. The little owl was associated with the Greek goddess Athene, who was often shown with an owl head. In some parts of the world, people believe that the soul becomes joined to an owl after death.

An ancient sport

Humans have used birds of prey to help them hunt for at least 4000 years. This is the sport of falconry. It probably started in China around 2000 BC. Birds of prey are tamed and trained to sit fly from their trainer's hand to kill birds or mammals for a small reward of fresh meat.

The falconer's hand is protected against the bird's talons by a tough leather glove. When not actually hunting a hood is fitted over the bird's face so that it is not distracted by other animals, cars, and so on. Bells may be attached so that the falconer can hear where it is.

Many different birds of prey are used in falconry. Peregrines are prized for their high speed, but the largest, fastest and most beautiful falcons are the gyrfalcons. The really big birds of prey, the eagles, are difficult to train and to keep in good flying condition.

▲ Birds of prey are carved on this original totem pole from Pacific Rim Park, Canada.

◄ A falconer with his tame African hawk eagle.

Helping airplanes

Falconers are employed by some airports to keep the runways free from birds. They are more successful than rook scarers, and do not harm the birds. The sight of a hawk or falcon simply makes them fly for cover.

More about ⟫ Falcons p 7-9, 11, 15, 21, 22, 26, 27, 32, 33, 37, 42-44, 49
Owls p 6-16, 18-20, 26, 28-34, 38, 40-46, 49, 50, 52, 54, 55 Bird of prey on flag p 41

The birds in this book

Common name	Distribution	Common name	Distribution
African hawk eagle	Africa	honey buzzard	Europe, Asia, Indonesia
American kestrel	N. and S. America	imperial eagle	S. Europe, Asia
Andean condor	S. America	king vulture	Central and S. America
bald eagle	Central America	lammergeier	Europe, Africa, Asia
barn owl	Most parts of the world	lanner falcon	S. Europe, Africa
bat falcon	Central and S. America	lappet-faced vulture	Africa
bat hawk	Asia, New Guinea, Africa	laughing falcons	Central and S. America
bateleur eagle	Africa	laughing owl	New Zealand
bay owl	Asia, Indonesia, Africa	little owl	Europe, Asia, N. Africa
bee-eater, European	Europe, Asia, N. Africa	long-eared owl	N. America, Europe, Asia N. Africa
black kite	Europe, Africa, Asia, Australasia	martial eagle	Africa
black vulture	N., Central and S. America	Mauritius kestrel	Mauritius
Bonelli's eagle	S. Europe, S. Asia, Africa	merlin/pigeon hawk	N. and S. America, N. Africa
boreal owl	*see* Tengmalm's owl	monkey-eating eagle	Philippines
burrowing owl	N., Central and S. America	Montagu's harrier	Europe, Asia, Africa
California condor	N. America	osprey	Worldwide
common buzzard	Europe, Asia, W. Africa	palm nut vulture	Africa
common caracara	S. USA, Central and S. America	peregrine/duck hawk	Worldwide
common kestrel	Europe, Asia, Africa	pink-backed pelicans	Africa, Arabia
common kingfisher	Europe, Asia, Africa	pygmy owl	Europe, Asia, N., Central and S. America
common tern	N. America, Europe, Asia, N. Africa	red kite	Asia, N. Africa
crane hawk	Central and S. America	red-tailed hawk	N. and Central America
crow	Europe	rook	Europe, Asia, N. Africa
eagle owl	Europe, Asia, N. Africa	savanna hawks	Central and S. America
Egyptian vulture	S. Europe, Africa, Asia	saw whet owl	N. America
elf owl	N. and Central America	screech owl	N. America
falconets	various	sea eagles	Europe, Asia, Africa, N. America
fish eagle	Africa, Asia, N. America	secretary bird	Africa
fishing eagles	Asia, Indonesia, Philippines	sharp-shinned hawk	N., Central and S. America
fishing owls	Asia, Indonesia, Africa	short-eared owls	Worldwide
forest falcons	Central and S. America	short-toed eagle	Europe, Asia, Africa, Indonesia
frigatebird	Indian and Pacific Oceans, Caribbean	snail kite	Florida, Central and S. America
gabar goshawk	Africa, Arabia	snake eagles	Africa
gannet	N. Atlantic coasts	snowy owl	N. America, Europe, Asia
golden eagle	N. America, Europe, Asia	sparrowhawk, European	Europe, Asia, Africa
goshawk	N. America, Europe, Asia	spotted eagles	Europe, Asia, Africa
gray heron	Europe, Asia, Africa	Swainson's hawk	N., Central and S. America
great gray owl	N. America, Europe, Asia	steppe buzzards	*see* common buzzard
great gray shrike	Europe, Asia, N. Africa	steppe eagles	Europe, Asia, Africa
griffon vulture	Europe, N. Africa, Asia	swallow-tailed kite	N., Central and S. America
gyrfalcon	N. America, Europe, Asia	tawny owl	Europe, Asia, N. Africa
harpy eagle	Central and S. America	Tengmalm's owl	N. America, N. Europe, N. Asia
harrier hawk	Madagascar	turkey vultures	N., Central and S. America
hen harrier	N. America, Europe, Asia	white-backed vulture	Africa
herring gull	N. America, Europe, Asia	white-tailed buzzard	Texas, Central and S. America
hobby	Europe, Asia, Africa		

Bibliography

Spotter's Guide to Birds of Prey, PETER HOLDEN AND RICHARD PORTER, Usborne, 1981.

British Birds of Prey, LESLIE BROWN, New Naturalist series, Collins, 1977.

The Encyclopaedia of Birds, Ed. Dr. Christopher Perrins and Dr. Alex Middleton, Unwin Animal Library, 1985.

Birds of Mountain and Moorland, Ed.John Gooders, Orbis Publishing, 1979.

Birds of Heath and Woodland, Ed. John Gooders, Orbis Publishing, 1979.

Owls, JOHN SPARKS AND TONY SOPER, David and Charles, 1978.

Bird Behaviour, ROBERT BURTON, Granada Publishing, 1985.

Bird Migration, CHRIS MEAD, Country Life Books, 1983.

Investigating bird pellets

The Amateur Naturalist, GERALD DURRELL, Hamish Hamilton, 1982.

The Family Naturalist, MICHAEL CHINERY, Macdonald and Jane's, 1977.

The Identification of Remains in Owl Pellets, D.W.YALDEN, Mammal Society, 1977.

Endangered birds

Save the Birds, ANTHONY W. DIAMOND, RUDOLF L. SCHREIBER, DAVID ATTENBOROUGH AND IAN PRESTT, Cambridge University Press, 1987.

Glossary

binocular vision: the use of both eyes to look at the same object. If the eyes are at the front of the head, their fields of view overlap. Each eye looks at the object from a different angle, so two different pictures are seen. From this information, the brain can work out how far away the object is. This is important for judging distance and speed.

birds of prey: birds that kill and eat other animals, especially birds with powerful feet and talons for grasping and killing, and hooked beaks for tearing flesh.

carrion: dead flesh.

cere: a featherless patch of skin at the base of the beak.

condors: large vultures found in North and South America.

cones: special cone-shaped light sensors in the eye that detect the color of the light.

crop: a pouch-like part of a bird's gullet, used to store food.

facial disks: flattened disks of feathers around a bird's eyes, thought to act as sound receptors.

fovea: an area of very densely-packed cones at the back of the eye. This is the point where the image falls when looking straight ahead. It gives the sharpest image.

gliding: flying by riding the air currents without flapping the wings. (The wings are held outstretched.)

incubate: to keep warm.

mandible: upper or lower part of a bird's beak.

migration: regularly traveling long distances between two particular places, usually along a particular route. Migration is often seasonal.

mobbing: the attacking of a larger bird by a smaller bird or birds in an attempt to drive it away.

nictitating membrane: a third, semi-transparent eyelid.

pellet: a regurgitated ball of undigested food remains.

predators: animals that hunt and kill other animals.

prey: animals that are hunted and killed by other animals.

pupil: the dark circle in the center of the eye, which is actually the gap in the iris through which light passes into the eye.

regurgitate: to bring back food into the mouth.

retina: the light-senstivie layer at the back of the eye.

roost: to sleep.

soaring: flying by gliding for long distances using rising air currents to prevent the bird from sinking.

still hunting: hunting by swooping down on prey from a look-out perch.

streamlined: shaped to give minimum resistance to air or water during locomotion. This usually involves having a body shape which is pointed or rounded at the head end, tapering to a thinner shape at the back.

talons: large claws.

territory: an area of land in which an animal or group of animals lives, feeds and/or breeds.

thermal: a rising current of warm air.

tundra: a vast expanse of treeless land in the far north where the soil is permanently frozen not far below the ground surface.

Index

Acknowledgments

ARTISTS:

David Anstey; Steve Lings/Linden Artists; Mick Loates/Linden Artists; Sallie Alane Reason; Helen Townson.

PHOTOGRAPHIC CREDITS:

t = top; b = bottom; c = centre; l = left; r = right.

COVER: John Shaw/NHPA. 6t Jeff Foot/Survival Anglia. 6b H. Schrempp/Frank Lane Picture Agency. 7 Colin Willock/Survival Anglia. 8 R. Austing/Frank Lane Picture Agency. 9 Gordon Langsbury/Bruce Coleman Ltd. 10 David T. Grewcock/Frank Lane Picture Agency. 11t David Hosking. 11b J. Pearson/Bruce Coleman Ltd. 12 Haroldo Palo, Jr./NHPA. 13 Andy Purcell/Bruce Coleman Ltd. 14 Richard and Julia Kemp/Survival Anglia. 15l M.P.L. Fogden/Bruce Coleman Ltd. 15r Godfrey Merlen/OSF. 17 Richard and Julia Kemp/Survival Anglia. 18 Rod Williams/Bruce Coleman Ltd. 19l Hans Reinhard/Bruce Coleman Ltd. 19r David Fox/OSF. 20 Kim Taylor/Bruce Coleman Ltd. 21 L. Campbell. NHPA. 22 Jonathon Scott/Seaphot. 23 Eric and David Hosking. 24 Jonathon Scott/Seaphot. 25l Rod Williams/Bruce Coleman Ltd. 25r Mike Price/Survival Anglia. 28t Leonard Lee Rue II/Frank Lane Picture Agency. 28b Brian Hawkes/NHPA. 29 Frank Lane Picture Agency. 30 Heinz Schrempp/Frank Lane Picture Agency. 31t Avril Ramage/OSF. 31l David Thompson/OSF. 31r Kim Taylor/Bruce Coleman Ltd. 33l John Jeffrey/NHPA. 33r Joe McDonald/Animals Animals/OSF. 34 Hellio and van Inge/NHPA. 35t N.G. Blake/Bruce Coleman Ltd. 35b Gunter Ziesler/Bruce Coleman Ltd. 36t Keith Scholey/Seaphot. 36b Sean T. Avery/Seaphot. 37t Josef Mihok/Survival Anglia. 37b J.L.G. Grande/Bruce Coleman Ltd. 38 Jonathon Scott/Seaphot. 39 Roger Tidman/NHPA. 40t Ray F. Bird/Frank Lane Picture Agency. 40b Jane Burton/Bruce Coleman Ltd. 42t Josef Mihok/Survival Anglia. 42b John Grerlach/Animals Animals/OSF. 43l Peter Johnson/NHPA. 43r Lewis W. Walker/Frank Lane Picture Agency. 44 Dennis Green/Survival Anglia. 46 J.L.G. Grande/Bruce Coleman Ltd. 47t Andy Purcell/Bruce Coleman Ltd. 47b Charles Palek/Animals Animals/OSF. 48t J.L.G. Grande/Bruce Coleman Ltd. 48b Jan and Des Barlett/Bruce Coleman Ltd. 49 R. Austing/Frank Lane Picture Agency. 51t Jeff Foott/Bruce Coleman Ltd. 51b S. Krasemann/NHPA. 52t George Edward/Survival Anglia. 52b J. Mihok/Survival Anglia. 53t M.P. Price/Bruce Coleman Ltd. 53b Eric and David Hosking. 54t Gunter Ziesler.Bruce Coleman Ltd. 54b M.A. Chappell/Animals Animals.OSF. 55 Christian Zuber. 56l Eric and David Hosking. 56r Jeff Foot/Survival Anglia.